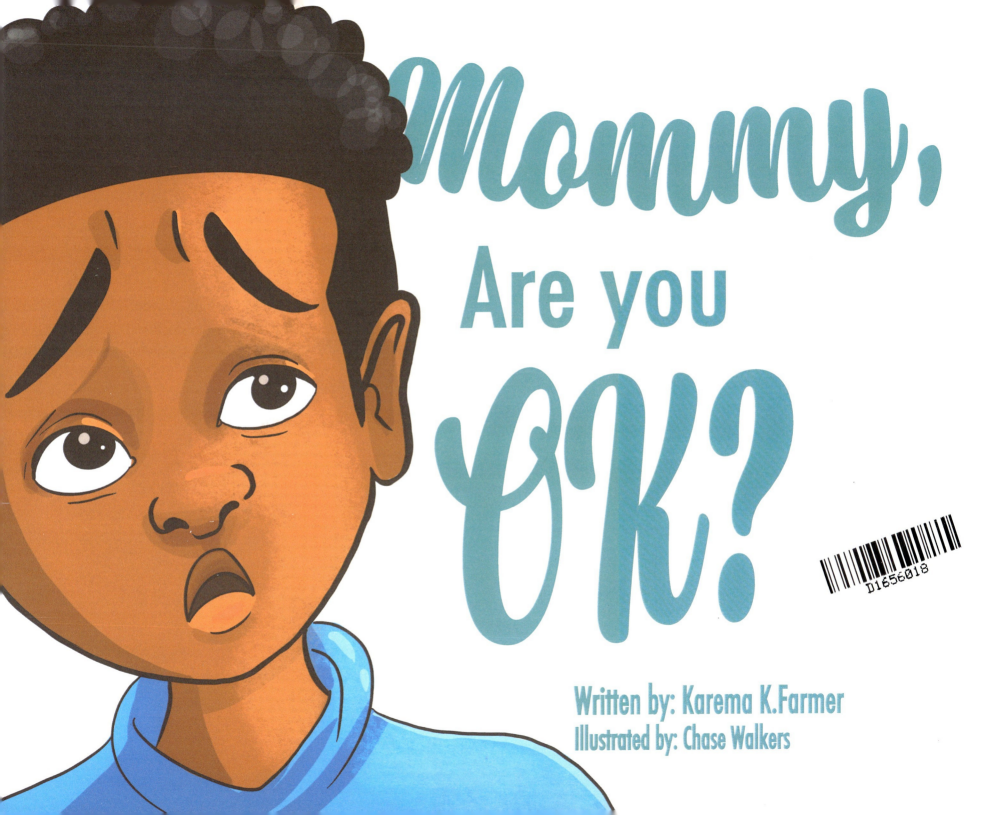

Mommy, Are You Ok?
Copyright © 2021 Karema K. Farmer
All Rights Reserved. Manufactured in the United States of America
No part of this publication may be used or reproduced in any manner without written permission of the author except in brief quotations embodied in critical articles and reviews.

For information address
Small House Publishing
22 Baily Road
Yeadon, PA 19050

www.smallhousepublishing.com
www.karemafarmer.com

ISBN: 978-1-7438427-3-9
Library of Congress Control Number: 2021903129

First Edition

Mommy, Are You OK? is dedicated to all new mothers and their families who are dealing with emotional changes after a baby's birth.

To be a new mother, especially in a home with multiple children, can be very overwhelming at times. Sometimes you cannot explain what is wrong and/or what can be done to help make things better. Please know, your feelings are valid and there are some things that can be done as a family to help you get through the emotional roller coaster caused by postpartum depression.

Mommies... I hear you. I see you. You are not alone.

Families... It is not your fault! You still matter. Please have patience.

Always remember, it is OK to not be OK.

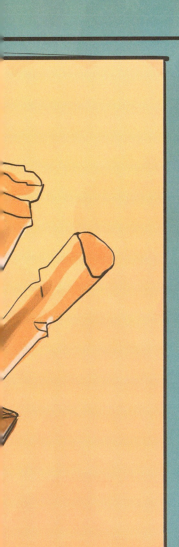

I'm so excited because I'll be a big brother soon.
Mommy and Daddy have been busy lately fixing up the baby's room.
Sometimes they let me help with the little things. Like organize the teddy bears or test out the baby's swing.

Mommy says the baby will be here in just a little while.
I can't wait to make my brother or sister laugh and smile.
I went and stayed with Grammy for just a few short days.
We played our favorite card games, and I always had the ace.

Mommy and Daddy are on their way home—I missed them so much!
I couldn't wait to hug them and the baby with a gentle touch.
When the car pulled into the driveway, I squealed with joy.
I will be so happy whether it's a girl or a boy!

"It's a boy!" Grammy told me as they entered the door.
"You're going to be a great big brother—I am very sure."
Oh, the fun we will have when he's old enough for us to play with each other!
We will go on many great adventures and learn new things together.

But something is different.
Mommy doesn't seem as happy as she used to be.
I must have done something wrong—maybe she's mad at me.
"Mommy, are you OK? Did I make you mad?"
Is there something I could do to make your heart glad?"

"Kevin, sometimes Mommies get sad, too," Daddy whispered quietly.
As he came over and hugged me very tightly.
"Why is she sad?" I thought, "Didn't she just have a baby?"
I know just what to do to cheer her up—maybe.

So, I hopped around the room and made a funny face.
Instead of laughing like before, she just stared off into space.
I told her all my best funny jokes, but that didn't seem to matter.
She gave me a little grin, but she still wasn't better.

When Grammy saw what I was doing, she came to sit with me.
"Sometimes, Mommies don't feel well after having a new baby."
She told me that there was nothing that anyone did to make Mommy sad.
And that Mommy will have some good days and some bad.

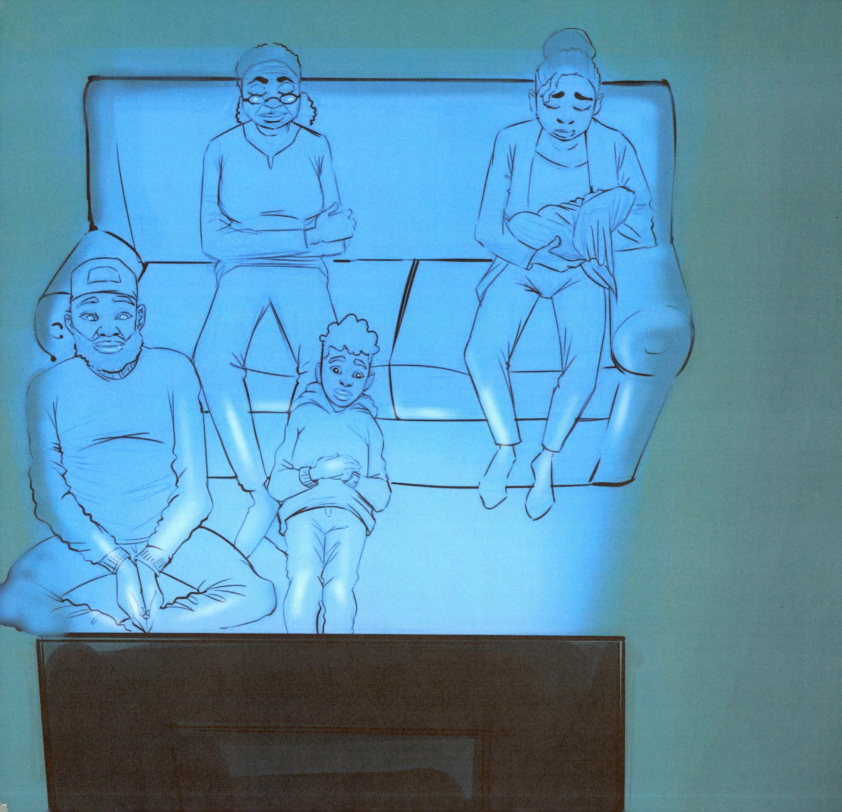

We just have to give her extra love and attention to help her feel glad.
And to remember to do all the things she likes when she is feeling sad.
"Don't play too loud or act too wild," Grammy cautiously warned me.
As we sat in the room with Mommy and watched her favorite
funny movie.

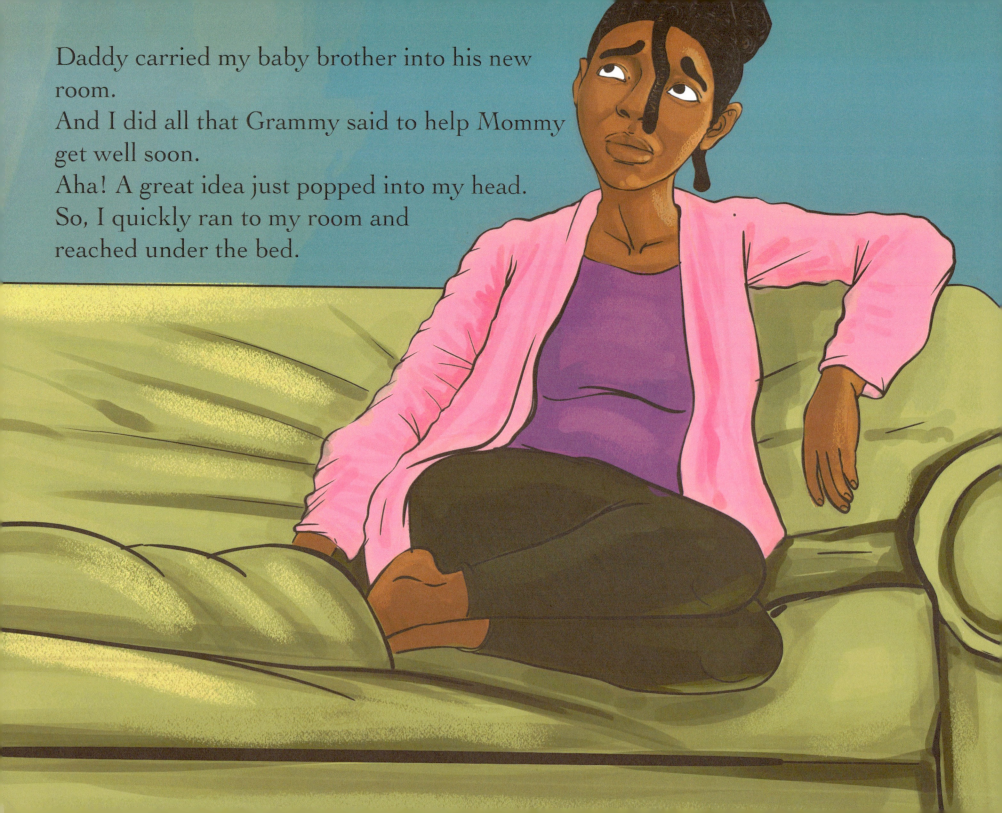

Daddy carried my baby brother into his new room.
And I did all that Grammy said to help Mommy get well soon.
Aha! A great idea just popped into my head.
So, I quickly ran to my room and reached under the bed.

I pulled out my special paper and pencil to write Mommy a letter.
To tell her how much I loved her and how I hope she feels better.
"I know this will do the trick!" I thought, "She will start smiling."
She always loves my drawings and my creative writing.

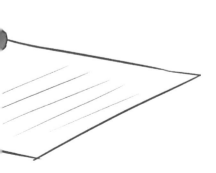

She read my letter slowly, and her mood began to change.
She then lifted her head to look at me and said the sweetest thing.
"My son, you are perfect. Thank you for being so kind.
I know it is hard for you to see me like this, but I will get better in time.
It is a little tough for me right now, but I will make it through.
Especially with a wonderful family and a caring son like you."

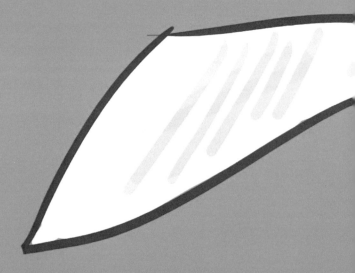

About the Author

Born and raised in the heart of Philadelphia, PA, Karema K. Farmer has always been a lover of the arts and creative expression. Karema captivates the heart of her audience by pouring out every ounce of her God-given talents through singing, poetry, spoken word, and other artistic mediums.

By profession, Karema is a Registered Nurse and Owner/Instructor of Incorporate Health, where she provides CPR training. Although she was blessed with the skills and desire to heal, she has ventured into her passion for storytelling. Through her work as a nurse and as an alumnus of Philadelphia High School for Creative and Performing Arts, she understands the importance of connecting and relating to people in all areas of their lives.

Karema's dream is to positively impact as many lives as possible and inspire the masses through her endeavors.

CPSIA information can be obtained
at www.ICGtesting.com
Printed in the USA
BVRC101020270521
608291BV00011B/420